This book belongs to
_____

Copyright © 2020 by Humor Heals Us. All rights reserved. No part of this book may be reproduced in any form without permission in writing from the publisher. Please send bulk order requests to Humorhealsus@gmail.com Printed and bound in the USA. 978-1-953399-12-0 Humorhealsus.com

On Christmas Eve, Santa gathered his reindeer together to leave for the big night.

They had many children to visit and Santa looked forward to the evening with his hard working reindeer.

Next was Cathleen Brooke. She was having a hard time at school because she had just moved there.

Everything was going smoothly until Rudolph's red nose stopped shining and Santa had no way of knowing if he was going the right way.

Before you knew it, he had landed in Antarctica where no children lived.

Everyone looked at each other without any ideas. Finally, Cupid came up with one.

So they took off with the torch. Cupid's plan was going well.

Santa felt crushed. He knew so many kids were depending on him. But without any light, he wasn't going to be able to finish his routes.

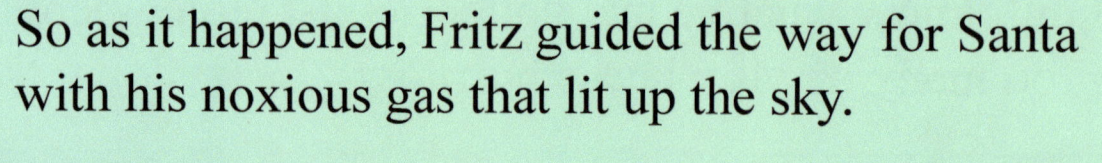

So as it happened, Fritz guided the way for Santa with his noxious gas that lit up the sky.

While Santa busy, the reindeers encouraged Fritz to snack as much as he could.

With boundless energy, Fritz lit up the sky for Santa. They visited every town and country, both big and small.

www.ingramcontent.com/pod-product-compliance
Lightning Source LLC
Chambersburg PA
CBHW041802290426
43673CB00099B/399